In memory of Julia Embrey Ingram
who taught me about a mother's unconditional love
for her children

25% of all proceeds will go to Angel Missions Haiti

Published by
Innovo Publishing, LLC
www.innovopublishing.com
1-888-546-2111

Innovo
Publishing

Providing Full-Service Publishing Services for
Christian Organizations & Authors: Hardbacks, Paperbacks,
eBooks, Audio Books, & iPhone/iPad Application Books

My Little Brother Chrisno
Copyright © 2010 by Drake Gunnell and Darlene Gunnell
All rights reserved.

ISBN 13: 978-1-936076-22-2
ISBN 10: 1-936076-22-5

Cover Design and Interior Design by Drake Gunnell and Darlene Gunnell

Printed in the United States of America
U.S. Printing History

First Edition: May 2010

Chrisno and Drake

My name is Drake Gunnell and this is my story about my little brother Chrisno.

Chrisno is from
another country called Haiti.
Haiti is very different
from where I live in Ringgold, Virginia.
Haiti is below America on the map.
Haiti is a very hot place
compared to here
in Virginia.
Haiti does not have many jobs,
so a lot of people do not have
a place to work.

America

HAITI

by Drake Gunnell
7/09

3

The Haitian people speak a different language called Creole. They eat a lot of rice and beans and most days only get to eat one meal. They also don't have clean water to drink. They do not have public schools so only a few children get to go to school. Not all people can get medical care, and this is why Chrisno came to America.

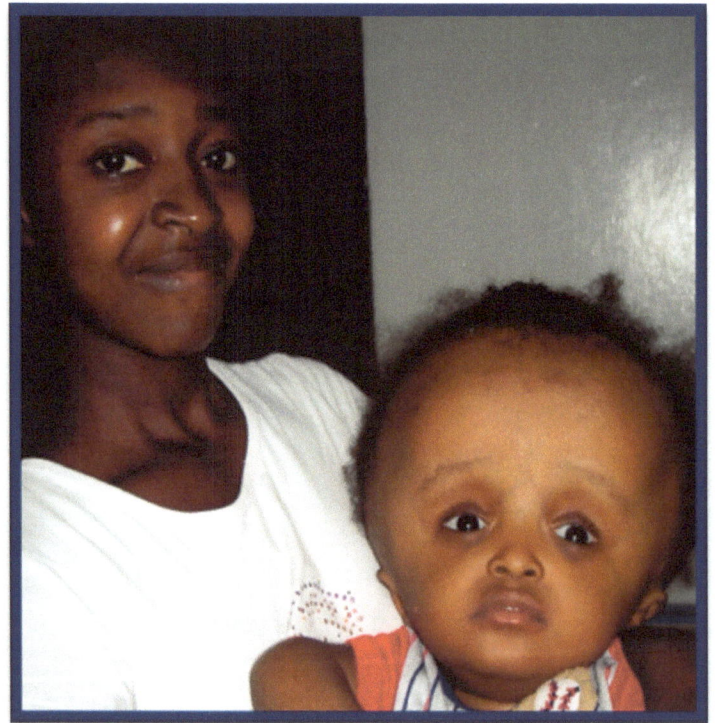

Joana Jeudi (Chrisno's mom) and Chrisno
Photo courtesy of AMH

Vanessa Carpenter (Mama V) of Angel Missions Haiti
Photo courtesy of AMH

Chrisno's Haitian mom, Joana Jeudi, noticed his head was getting very big and she took him to a medical clinic set up by Angel Missions Haiti in the city of Port-au-Prince. An American woman named Vanessa Carpenter, also called Mama V by the Haitian people, started the clinic to help the children of Haiti get the medical care they need for free.

5

Chrisno's head was getting bigger because the fluid in his head was not draining right. My mom said we all have fluid around our brain and the fluid runs down into our bodies. Chrisno needed surgery to drain the fluid off his brain. Mama V knew this could not be done in Haiti. Chrisno would not be able to live long and would be in a lot of pain if someone didn't help him.

Mama V found a hospital in the United States and two doctors willing to help Chrisno. The hospital was Carilion Clinic Children's Hospital in Roanoke, Virginia. Dr. Lisa Apfel would do the surgery and Dr. Kitty Humphreys would be his baby doctor.

Carilion Clinic Children's Hospital, a member of Children's Miracle Network

Photo courtesy of Carilion Hospital

Mama V then needed a family to keep Chrisno while he came to the United States for surgery. My mom saw Mama V on TV asking for someone to take Chrisno in for 3 to 4 months. Mom and Dad decided to help. They called Mama V and told her Chrisno could stay with us.

My oldest brother Drew was 12 years old, my other brother Derrick was 10 years old, and I was 6 years old when Chrisno came to stay with us, but I turned seven after he got here. Chrisno turned 2 while he was with us.

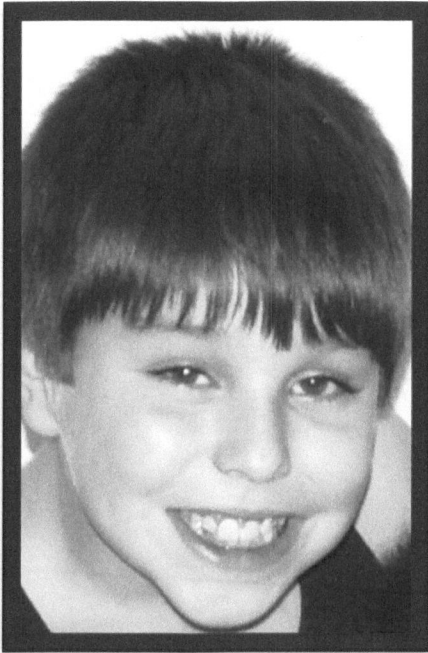  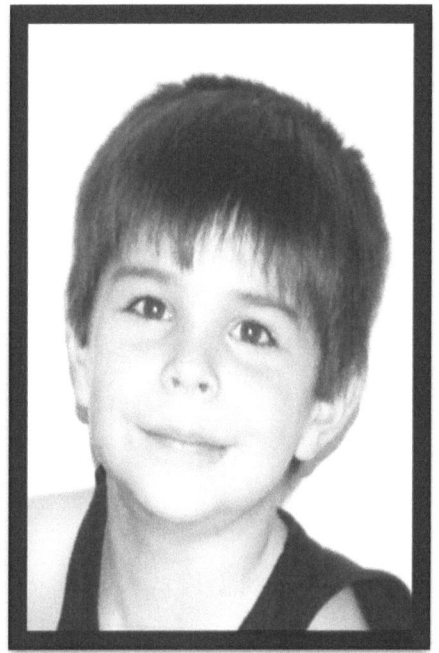

Derrick   Drew   Drake

My Mom met Mama V in Roanoke to pick Chrisno up while I was at school. When I saw him, I wondered how his head could be so big. He had to sit in the car seat all the time for his head to be held up because he couldn't hold it up by himself. Chrisno was fussy. Mom said he was probably scared and wanted his mommy back in Haiti. I tried talking to him to get him to stop crying but he wouldn't. Mom said he couldn't understand what I was saying because in his country they do not speak English.

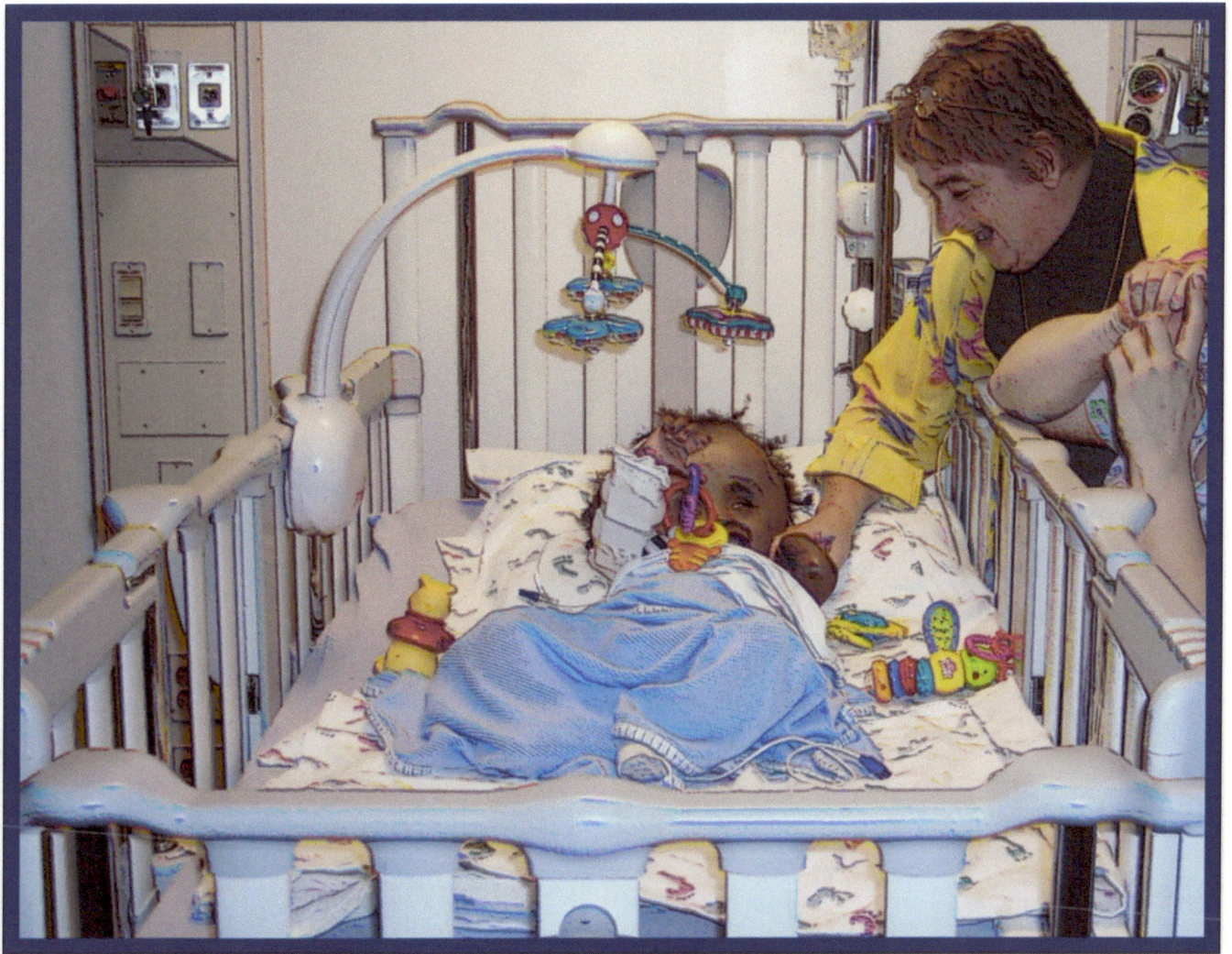

Picture courtesy of AMH

Chrisno stayed at the hospital for a few days to have the surgery. Dr. Apfel put something called a shunt (a tube) in his head to get the fluid out. The tube runs down the back of his neck into his stomach. My mom said his head would stay big because his bones had hardened into that shape.

When Chrisno came back to our house, he started feeling better and getting used to us. I would play with him every day when I got home from school. I would help my mom feed him his bottle too.

My brother Drew would play the guitar for Chrisno.

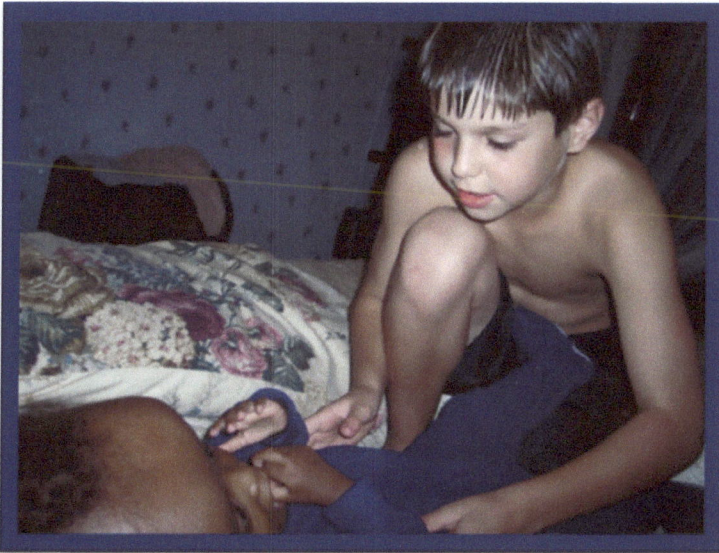

My other brother Derrick would make sounds to try to get Chrisno to laugh.

Chrisno has such a funny laugh. He would make all of us laugh when he laughed. Every day when my brothers and I got off the bus, we'd race into the house to be the first to play with him.

Chrisno started doing a lot of things he couldn't do before. He started to roll onto his side. He'd pull the blanket up over his head, and if I said, "Where's Chrisno?" he would pull it down and laugh. He started eating chicken nuggets and french fries, too, just like I do.

Chrisno still couldn't sit up, though, because his head was too heavy. So my Mom, who is a Physical Therapist Assistant, asked a friend of hers who makes braces, named Doug Smiley, if he could make a brace to help Chrisno hold his head up.

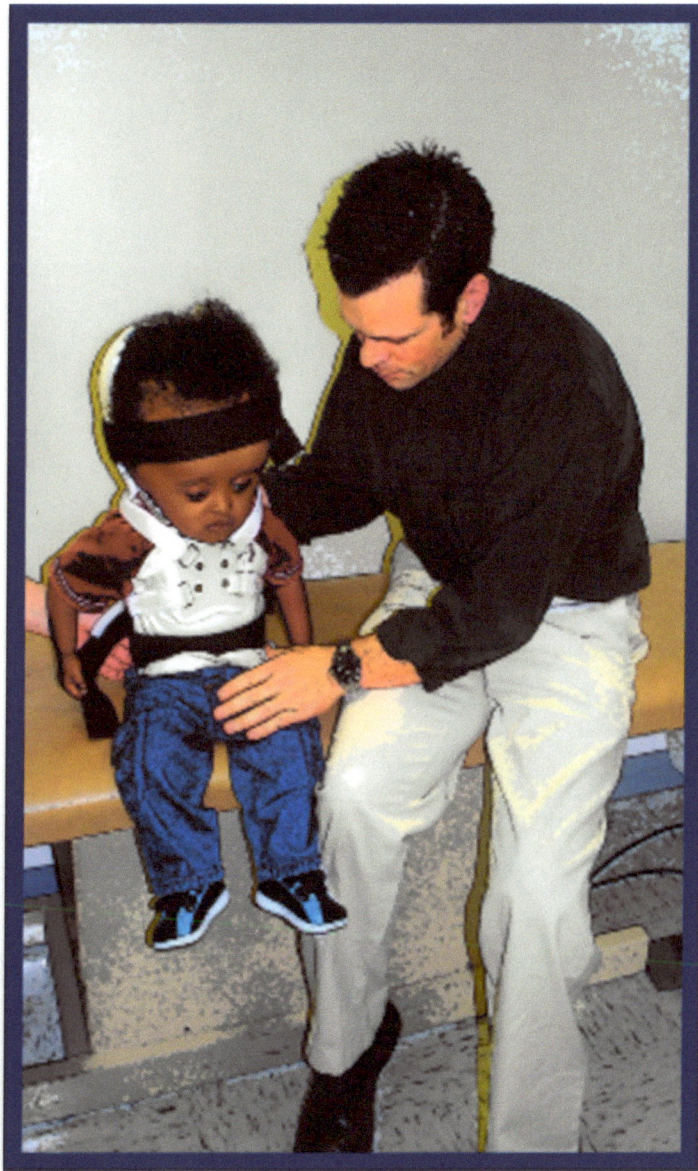

Chrisno and Doug Smiley of Virginia Prosthetics

Mr. Smiley made Chrisno a brace. With his brace on, Chrisno was able to sit in a high chair to feed himself...

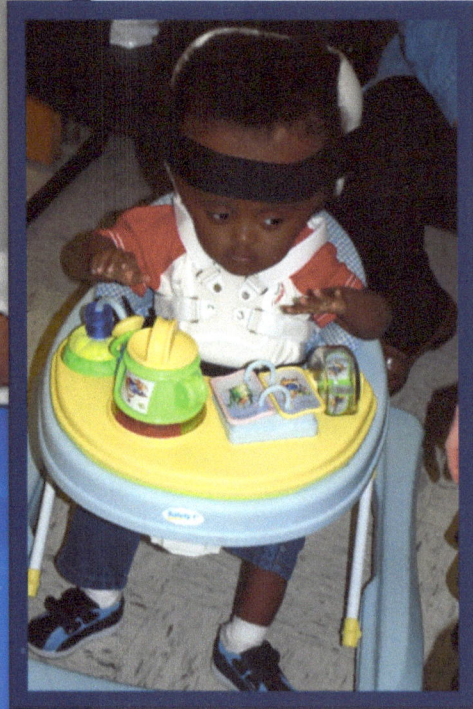

...and he was able to start walking in a baby walker.

My Mom said, "Chrisno's body just needs to grow until he can hold his head up without any help." He stayed with us 4 months and then he went back home to his mom and dad. I didn't want him to go. Everyone in my family loved Chrisno, and he loved us too. We all wanted him to stay, but my Mom said his mom and dad missed him and were waiting for him to come home. We took Chrisno to Mama V's house in Salem, Virginia, and said goodbye. I felt like I was going to cry, but Mama V told me Chrisno's mommy was waiting for him to come back home and that she missed him very much.

Chrisno went back to Haiti to be with his parents. Then we heard that his mom and dad were not able to take him home because they could not provide for him in his condition. They wanted him to be somewhere he could have a place to sleep and a meal every day because they loved him so much. They were making the biggest sacrifice of their lives. This was their only child, their son. Just as God sacrificed His only Son for His children to have a better life with Him in Heaven, Mr. and Mrs. Jeudi had to make sacrifices so their son could have a better life than they could provide.

They were going to have to put Chrisno in an orphanage, a place children live when they don't have parents to take care of them. My parents talked to me and my brothers and they asked us if we would like for Chrisno to come back to live with us and be our brother. They explained to us that Chrisno's parents loved him, but they just couldn't take care of him. They told us Haiti was a very poor place without jobs and they didn't have a lot of food to eat. My Mom and Dad said that we could adopt Chrisno. They felt God had sent him to be with us, and we could help him have a full and happy life.

The Gunnell Family

William, Darlene, Drake, Derrick, Drew, and Chrisno

So this is how Chrisno became my little brother.

A true story
written by
Drake Gunnell and Darlene Gunnell

Special Thanks to
Vanessa and Tom Carpenter
Angel Missions Haiti
Virginia Prosthetics
All the staff of Carilion Clinic Children's Hospital
(a member hospital of children's Miracle Network)

And a very special thanks to . . .

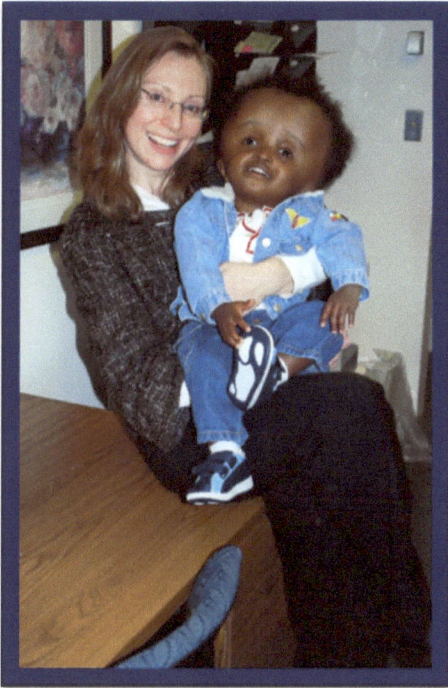

Dr. Lisa Apfel
Carilion Clinic Neurosurgery

Dr. Kitty Humphreys,
Village Family Physicians,
a division of Centra
Medical Group

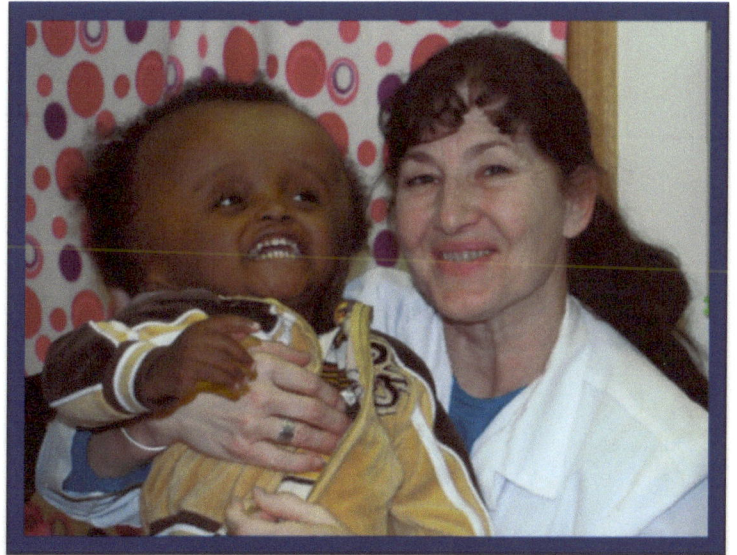